SCIENCE AND
GOVERNMENT

The Godkin Lectures at
Harvard University, 1960

The Godkin Lectures on the Essentials of Free Government and the Duties of the Citizen were established at Harvard University in memory of Edwin Lawrence Godkin (1831–1902).

SCIENCE AND GOVERNMENT

by C. P. Snow

HARVARD UNIVERSITY PRESS
1961   Cambridge, Massachusetts

Q
127
.G4
S62
1961

© Copyright 1960, 1961
by the President and Fellows of Harvard College

All rights reserved

Published in Great Britain
by Oxford University Press, London

Library of Congress Catalog Card Number: 61–7396
Printed in the United States of America

PREFACE

I should like to thank the President and Fellows of Harvard College for the honour of being asked to deliver these lectures.

Sections II–VIII (pp. 4–47) are concerned with a piece of recent history. For this, my main written sources have been the Tizard papers. As I have said in the text (p. 5), I am deeply grateful to Dr. Peter Tizard, Lady Tizard, and Mr. R. H. Tizard for the chance to study and use these sources: they are probably the richest of any in England connected with the scientific side of the 1939–45 war.

I have also had the good luck to be able to talk to many of the people who were involved in those events. The list of names would be too long to give here: but I owe a special debt to Dr. Noble Frankland, Historian of the Air Ministry and now Director of the Imperial War Museum, Dr. A. V. Hill, Professor P. M. S. Blackett, and Dr. A. P. Rowe.

During 1960 I happen to have spent some time in four of the great universities of the world: the English Cambridge, which of course I love; the Lomonosov University of Moscow; the University of California at Berke-

Preface

ley, which was kind enough to ask me to spend the autumn there; and Harvard. I have much feeling for all these institutions, and I do not relish praising one more than the others. And yet I felt again, as I came to Harvard for the third time, that this was in many ways the most splendid university I had ever set foot in. Giving three lectures on three successive nights is pretty rough on the lecturer, not to speak of his audience. That is what, as Godkin lecturer, I have just had to do. My impression of Harvard's splendour has survived the experience, and therefore, it seems to me, will remain with me for good.

C. P. S.

Leverett House, Cambridge
December 2, 1960

SCIENCE AND
GOVERNMENT

SCIENCE AND GOVERNMENT

{.sep} I.

One of the most bizarre features of any advanced industrial society in our time is that the cardinal choices have to be made by a handful of men: in secret: and, at least in legal form, by men who cannot have a firsthand knowledge of what those choices depend upon or what their results may be.

When I say "advanced industrial society" I am thinking in the first place of the three in which I am most interested—the United States, the Soviet Union, and my own country. And when I say the "cardinal choices," I mean those which determine in the crudest sense whether we live or die. For instance, the choice in England and the United States in 1940 and 1941, to go ahead with work on the fission bomb: the choice in 1945 to use that bomb when it was made: the choice in the United States and the Soviet Union, in the late forties, to make the fusion bomb: the choice, which led to a different result in the United States and the Soviet Union, about intercontinental missiles.

It is in the making of weapons of absolute destruction that you can see my central theme at its sharpest and most dramatic, or most melodramatic if you like.

2   *Science and Government*

But the same reflections would apply to a whole assembly of decisions which are not designed to do harm. For example, some of the most important choices about a nation's physical health are made, or not made, by a handful of men, in secret, and, again in legal form, by men who normally are not able to comprehend the arguments in depth.

This phenomenon of the modern world is, as I say, bizarre. We have got used to it, just as we have got used to so many results of the lack of communication between scientists and nonscientists, or of the increasing difficulty of the languages of science itself. Yet I think the phenomenon is worth examining. A good deal of the future may spring from it.

In the West, we have not been very good at looking at this singularity with fresh and candid eyes. We are too apt to delude ourselves with phrases like "the free world," or "the freedom of science." None of those phrases is meaningful when we are concerned with the kind of choice I am describing. Such phrases only obscure the truth. I shall come back to that point later. For the moment I will just say that all societies, whatever their political structure or legalistic formulations, are going to be faced with this same type of choice so long as we have nation-states, and that the results are going to be not only significant, but much too significant.

Science and Government

I know that we can draw diagrams of political responsibility which are able to make us feel that everything can be reconciled with the principles of parliamentary government. But if we do, we shall not even begin to understand what is really happening. We shall fool ourselves, as we do too often, with that particular brand of complacency, of lack of gravity, which is one of the liabilities of the West, growing upon us perhaps as we become more affluent.

The first thing, it seems to me, is to try to understand what really happens. "We must learn to think," Don K. Price has written, "without making use of the patterns or models taken for granted by most of the text books."[1] It is harder than it sounds.

No one who has ever thought at all about the relations of science and government, much less anyone who has experienced part of them directly, is likely to think that positive conclusions are going to be either firm or easy to come by. Most of the concepts that administrative theorists use are at best rationalisations, not guides to further thought; as a rule they are unrealistically remote from the workaday experience.

No one that I have read has found the right answers. Very few have even asked the right questions. The best I can do is tell a story. The story is intended to contain a little of something which actually did happen. I shall not pretend that the story is not sup-

4   *Science and Government*

posed to bear some relation to our present problems. I shall try to extract a few generalisations from it, or, to be more sensible, a few working rules.

II. ᠕᠕᠕᠕᠕᠕᠕᠕᠕᠕᠕᠕᠕᠕

This story is about two men and two choices. The first of the two men is Sir Henry Tizard. Let me declare my interest straight away, as they say in English board rooms. I believe, along with a number of Englishmen who are interested in recent military-scientific history, that Tizard's was the best scientific mind that in England has ever applied itself to war. I further believe, although in general I take a pretty Tolstoyan view of the influence of distinguished men upon events, that of all the people who had a share in England's surviving the air battles of July to September 1940, Tizard made a contribution at least as great as any. It has not yet been properly recognised. As he himself wrote in his diary on May 8th, 1945, when he was living in what for him was high-level exile, as president of Magdalen College, Oxford, "I wonder if the part that scientists have played will ever be faithfully and fully recorded. Probably not."[2]

To an American audience, it is natural that I should

Science and Government 5

have to introduce him from scratch: but if I was speaking of him to most English audiences, I should have to do the same. In fact I have never spoken of him before, and I am very glad that I should do so for the first time in the United States. He had much feeling for America and American science. It was owing to him, as we shall see, that, sixteen months before the United States came into the war, American scientists were told all that the English were doing and all they knew. That gesture of bold trust, forced through by him, and very like his temperament, saved both our countries quite an appreciable bit of time in the Hitler war.

I happen to know that he would have liked me to talk about him, because I once threatened him with it. He said: "At least I can trust you to do it with the gloves off." He meant, of course, as he said himself when writing of Rutherford, that with characters big enough one ought not to be polite. His family are also sure that he would have relished being treated so, and I have been given unqualified access to the Tizard papers. He wrote quite a lot about himself. He began an autobiography and he kept a number of fragmentary diaries. Towards the end of his life, like a good many men who have played a part in history, he wanted his own end of the record to be kept straight. Although I knew him well, I have drawn on this

6   *Science and Government*

documentary material as well as on other written sources. There is very little in what follows which is my own opinion or unsupported impression. When there is, I shall try to make it clear.

What was he like? Physically he did not alter much from middle age, when I first met him, until he died in 1959. He was English of the English. His whole appearance, build, and manner were something one does not often see outside England, or even outside the English professional class from which he sprang. He was not pretty. There were times when he looked like a highly intelligent and sensitive frog. His hair, what was left of it, was reddish. His face was unusually wide across the jaw line. But his expression was transfigured by his eyes, which were transparent light blue, sparkling with dash and interest. He was middle sized, and like nearly all successful men of affairs, he was in a muscular sense strong. But that tough physique, that alert, confident, commanding manner, that warm rasp of a voice, hid certain disharmonies. He was not all of a piece.

He came into a room, and he had an authority, a pugnacity, that made men attend to him. He had a lively satirical tongue, of a kind that seemed a little stylised to my generation. "Andrade [who was looking after wartime inventions] is like an inverted Micawber, waiting for something to turn down." Of the personal

Science and Government

antagonism with which I shall soon be dealing: "The hatchet is buried for the present: but the handle is conveniently near the surface." And so on. There were heaps of Tizardisms—but they were to an extent misleading.

True, he knew he was a gifted man; he knew his own capacity pretty well; but the confidence which made men follow him was not the deep-rooted, relaxed confidence of those who have their creative achievement safely behind them—the relaxed creative confidence, for example, of his idol Rutherford. Tizard did not always find himself easy to live with. The bold face he put on did not completely mask the strains of his inner life.

In the same way, his tough powerful physique was not as impregnable as it looked. All his life he seems to have been vulnerable to infections, suddenly knocked out by mysterious high temperatures. He was lucky in his family, and had sons of very high ability: but he had a great need for affection, not only in his family, but among his friends. Friendship mattered more to him than it would have done if he had been the self-sufficient man he looked. Fortunately for him, he had the energy and warmth to make friends of all ages. I sometimes thought he was at his happiest in the Athenaeum—he had the curious distinction of being able to make the Athenaeum cosy—among peo-

8   *Science and Government*

ple who not only admired him, but were fond of him.

He was born in 1885. His father was a naval officer —a naval officer of strong scientific leanings, who became assistant hydrographer to the Navy and a Fellow of the Royal Society, but first and foremost a naval officer. That had a direct importance to Tizard, both in his attitudes and in what he was able to achieve. All his life he had the simple, unquestioning, absolute patriotism of a regular officer: and he had a complete intuitive understanding of what soldiers and sailors were like. Except for a physical chance, in fact, he would have been one himself. He would—as a matter of course in such a family—have entered the Navy, if it had not been discovered, just before the examination, that he had a blind patch in one eye. Tizard says, "I must have taken this verdict philosophically at the time, for I don't remember being disappointed or relieved: but it was a bad blow for my father . . . He went to a friend in the Admiralty and said, 'What would you do with a boy who cannot get into the Navy?' "[3]

These traditional loyalties were very deep in Tizard. In scientific and technical things his mind was radical: but emotionally he remained until he died bound to that upright, intelligent, dutiful, conservative line. His family were always short of money. Running true to form of the conservative English service families, they both had a certain contempt for money and were con-

Science and Government 9

stantly worried about it. That stayed so with Tizard.
He was worried about money till his death. He never
made any, and when he retired from the public service
no proper provision was made for him, owing to the
changes and chances of his career. His one bitter com-
plaint, in his old age, was that he did not know how
he was going to live.

Instead of entering the Navy, he went through an
orthodox professional English education—Westmin-
ster and Oxford. He was dazzlingly clever at anything
he put his hand to. Later on he thought he might
have made a goodish academic mathematician, and
wished he had tried. Actually, he specialised in chemistry, which was at the time the only adequate scientific school in Oxford. Oxford is now, of course,
highly developed in scientific subjects, and it is a bit
startling to be reminded that the young Tizard in 1908,
bursting with both academic honours and promise,
anxious to make a start in research, could find no one
in Oxford to work under. Like other bright young
Englishmen and Americans of that period, he decided that Germany was the place to find the masters
of research. He went off to Berlin to work under
Nernst.

As it turned out, he did not bring off anything of
scientific interest during his year there. But he brought
off something else. For it was in Nernst's laboratory

10 *Science and Government*

that he first met the other main character in this story. There is a difficulty about this other character because of the English habit of changing names and styles. Thirty odd years later, as the right-hand man and grey eminence of Winston Churchill, he became known as Lord Cherwell. But nearly all the way through his friendship and enmity with Tizard he was called F. A. Lindemann. That is the name by which Tizard in his papers always refers to him. For clarity's sake I shall stick to the same convention.

III. ~~~~~~~~~~~~~~~~~~~

These two young men met in Berlin in the autumn of 1908. We do not know the exact circumstances. It would be nice to know, for even if we eliminate what was to happen, they were two of the most remarkable young men alive, and there cannot have been many such meetings. Lindemann was, by any standards, a very odd and a very gifted man, a genuine heavyweight of personality. I did not know him as well as I did Tizard, but I talked to him a good many times. As he thought I was relatively sensible about the job I was doing, he gave me some tough support. He even made a speech about me in the House of Lords.[4] More im-

Science and Government 11

portant than that, as far as I was concerned, his was
the sort of character that makes a novelist's fingers
itch. So, although in the two issues I am going to use
for analytical purposes I have no doubt that he was
wrong and Tizard right, I have a soft spot for him and
a complex of respect. I do not think that I should be
so interested in the Tizard-Lindemann struggles if I
did not have that kind of feeling for both men.

I said that Tizard was English of the English. Lindemann was quite un-English. If one met him for the
first time in middle age, I have always thought that
one would have taken him for a Central European
business man—pallid, heavy featured, correctly
dressed, one who had been a notable tennis player in
his youth and was now putting on weight. He spoke
German as well as he did English, and there was a
faint Teutonic undertone to his English, to his in-
audible, constricted mumble. No one seems to know
to this day what his father's nationality was.[5] He may
have been a German or an Alsatian. It is possible,
though I doubt it, that he was Jewish. No doubt this
rather silly mystery will be cleared up in the official
biography which Lord Birkenhead is now writing. But
it is certain that Lindemann's father was distinctly
rich, and Lindemann himself, unlike Tizard, had the
attitude to money of a rich man, not of a member of
the professional Establishment.

12 Science and Government

There was a similar sharp difference in the nature of their patriotism. As I have said, Tizard's was the patriotism of a naval officer, which came to him as naturally and unselfconsciously as breathing. Lindemann, who was not an Englishman but became one, had the fanatical patriotism of someone who adopts a country which is nevertheless not, in the deepest sense, his own. No one cared more about England than Lindemann, in his own way: but it was a way that, with its flavour of the patriotism of the converted exile, struck men like Tizard as uncomfortable and strained.

A great deal else of Lindemann's personality struck them also as uncomfortable and strained. About him there hung an air of indefinable malaise—so that, if one was drawn to him at all, one wanted to alleviate it. He was formidable, he was savage, he had a suspicious malevolent sadistic turn of what he would have called humour, though it was not really that. But he did not seem, when it came to the most fundamental things, to understand his own life, and despite his intelligence and will, he did not seem good at grappling with it. He enjoyed none of the sensual pleasures. He never drank. He was an extreme and cranky vegetarian, who lived largely on the whites of eggs, Port Salut cheese, and olive oil. So far as is known, he had no

Science and Government   13

sexual relations. And yet he was a man of intense emotions.

Tizard, whose emotions were also deep and difficult to control, had an outgoing nature, which, luckily for him, found him wife and family and friends. Lindemann's passions were repressed and turned in upon himself. You could hear the difference in their kind of joke. Tizard, as I mentioned, had a tongue which was harsh, which could be rough with pretentious persons, but which was in the long run goodnatured. Lindemann's had the bitter edge of repression.

I remember being in Oxford one morning when the Honours List had been published. I think this must have been during the war. I was talking to Lindemann. I happened to remark that the English honours system must cause far more pain than pleasure: that every January and June the pleasure to those who got awards was nothing like so great as the pain of those who did not. Miraculously Lindemann's sombre, heavy face lit up. His brown eyes were usually sad, but now they were glowing. With a gleeful sneer he said: "Of course it is. It wouldn't be any use getting an award if one didn't think of all the people who were miserable because they hadn't managed it."

In that kind of venom, in almost everything he did,

14   *Science and Government*

he was much more intense than most men. His passions were a bit bigger than life-size; they often took on the inflated monomania of the passions in Balzac's novels. He was altogether a bit bigger than life-size. As I have already said, he was a character who made a novelist's fingers itch. And yet, thinking of him and Tizard, I am not sure which would interest me more as a novelist. When I was younger, Lindemann certainly. Now that I have found my interest gradually change from what we call "abnormal" to "normal" personalities—I am using these words, of course, as a shorthand jargon—I think it might be Tizard. He was externally a far less odd man than Lindemann. In the structure of his personality he was probably more complex.

IV. ᴡᴡᴡᴡᴡᴡᴡᴡᴡᴡᴡᴡ

One would like to know what they talked about, in Berlin that winter of 1908. Science, of course. Both had an unshakable faith that science was the supreme intellectual manifestation of the mind of man, a faith they never lost. Tizard had strong interests in literature, but Lindemann none, nor in any other art. Maybe they talked about politics. Both were con-

Science and Government   15

servative, but Tizard had the receptive tolerant conservatism of the Establishment, while Lindemann was eccentrically, and often extremely, reactionary. I do not think they talked of love or young women, as men of that age might be expected to.

There was a romantic story, dear to some in Whitehall who met them in the days of their power and un-patch-up-able quarrels, that they had once been inseparable. I believe, from the quotation from Tizard's autobiography which follows and from other evidence, that that is overdoing it. It is true that Tizard was writing long after the event: but he was also deliberately composing his autobiography with the Lindemann feud as its chief dramatic conflict, and he was too much of a natural storyteller to have underplayed their original friendship, if honesty had not compelled him to do so.

F. A. Lindemann and I became close but not intimate friends. [This is the first reference to Lindemann in the autobiography.] There was always something about him which prevented intimacy. He was one of the cleverest men I have known. He had been to school in Germany, and talked German very well—as well as he talked English —and was fluent in French. He was a very good experimenter. He also played games well. He wanted me to share rooms with him [in Berlin] but I refused. I think my chief reasons for doing so at the time were that he was much better off than I was and I could hardly com-

16 *Science and Government*

pete with his standard of living, and also that we should be speaking English all the time, for he would take no trouble to teach me German. It was lucky that I refused because we had a minor row later on. I had discovered a gymnasium in Berlin which was run by an ex-lightweight champion boxer of England, so I used to go there for exercise. I persuaded Lindemann to join and box with me.

Now one of his greatest defects was that he hated anyone of his own age to excel him in anything. He was a clumsy and inexperienced boxer, and when he found that I, who was much shorter and lighter than he was, was much quicker with my hands and on my feet, he lost his temper completely, so much so that I refused to box with him again. I don't think he ever forgave me for that. Still, we remained close friends for over twenty-five years, but after 1936 he became a bitter enemy.[6]

After that year in Berlin, Lindemann stayed in Germany, where he had his entire education, high school, undergraduate, and postgraduate. Tizard returned to England and became a scientific don at Oxford. As he wrote himself,[7] in view of his subsequent career it was strange that he did not remember taking the slightest interest in the application of science to war before 1914. At that time, all his ambitions were in pure science, and they were broken only by the beginning of the war and by a friendship, a hero-worshipping friendship, with Rutherford. That sounds a paradox, since Rutherford was the supreme creative

Science and Government 17

expression of pure science, but it makes good psychological sense, and I will deal with it in a moment.

In the 1914–18 war both Tizard and Lindemann, in their early thirties, played picturesque parts. Both happened to be not only brave, but abnormally brave, in the starkest physical sense. Both happened to find their way into the primitive aircraft experimentation of the time. They volunteered for it, because they were not allowed to fight behind machine guns. Tizard was offered flying training, but only in weather *too rough* for the normal flying cadets. "Done," he said. Lindemann, for experimental purposes, deliberately put his aircraft into a spinning nosedive. It was against the statistical probabilities that either remained alive, let alone both.

After the war their lives interweaved again. Tizard went back to teach chemistry at Oxford. He put in a word with the electors to the chair of experimental philosophy on behalf of Lindemann,[8] who was duly elected, much to the astonishment of the English physicists, since Lindemann had never been inside an English university. Lindemann became godfather to one of Tizard's children. For two or three years it seemed that they might lead a scientific renaissance in Oxford, the first since the seventeenth century.

But then something began to happen to them both —quite clearly to Tizard, more foggily to Lindemann,

18   *Science and Government*

who had far less introspective insight. What happened was simple. They knew they were never going, by high standards, to make a success of pure science. Tizard was explicit about it, both in conversation, "I knew I should never be any *real* good," and in his autobiography, "I now convinced myself that I would never be outstanding as a pure scientist. Younger men were coming on of greater ability in that respect."[9] By this he meant that he could not fight at the same weight as Rutherford and his friends. Rutherford, who had become a major influence in his life, had set him a standard to judge scientific achievement by. Tizard did not expect to be a Rutherford. They occurred once in three hundred years. But he was a proud man, he had a sense of his own powers, and he wanted at least to be as good as the next rung down. He felt he was not, and that settled it.

In all this I am reminded of Alfred Kazin's comment about Englishmen weighing themselves and each other up as though they were so much horseflesh. All I can say is, it happened. With Lindemann, it took more time, and it was not so incisive. But he was an even prouder man than Tizard, and internally more convinced that he had a great intellect. He could not tolerate not being able to compete on the one hand with Rutherford and the new generation of Rutherford's pupils, Chadwick, Cockcroft, Kapitza, Blackett,

Science and Government   19

or, on the side of mathematical physics, with Bohr, Heisenberg, Dirac, and a dozen others. It just wasn't good enough. So they each, one consciously and the other gropingly, took their separate ways out.

It is interesting to wonder whether they were right. If they had had more creative confidence, which they both seriously lacked, would they have left a real scientific memorial behind them? After all, they were out of comparison more intelligent than many scientists who have made major discoveries. In his last years Tizard certainly—here I cannot speak for Lindemann —would have given up all his other achievements if he could have had even a quarter of a Rutherfordian oeuvre to his credit. With more luck, with less pride, could he, could either of them, have done it? As I think that, I hear, from twenty years ago, the clear voice of G. H. Hardy: "For anything worth doing [by which Hardy meant creative work, which he took for granted was the only thing worth doing] intelligence is a very minor gift."

Probably, one is forced to believe, their intelligence would not have compensated, and they were right when they contracted out. Tizard had a very broad scientific comprehension. He was the kind of scientist, of which Willard Gibbs was a supreme example, who builds great systems: but Tizard had not the special insight which would have let him see which sys-

20　　*Science and Government*

tem, in his own time, was there to be built. Lindemann was the opposite. Apart from his zest in destructive criticism, he was a gadgety scientist, inventive, on the lookout for ingenious tricks. To make use of that gadgety talent, one has to have the obsessive force that can keep one thinking over one device for year after year. Aston could do that, so could C. T. R. Wilson, so could Thomas Merton.[10] But Lindemann soon got tired. That was why he remained an amateur among professionals: which, by the way, was how the leaders of physics, such as Rutherford, always regarded him.

V. 〰〰〰〰〰〰〰〰

So, though they both became fellows of the Royal Society at an early age—earlier than they could have hoped to become in the conditions of today—Tizard and Lindemann slipped out of pure science. And their ways of slipping out brought about the two great collisions. Tizard became a high-level scientific administrator. That was less than forty years ago, but England had only just begun to spend money on applied science. It was during the 1914–18 war that the Department of Scientific and Industrial Research was started. Tizard, who had made a great reputation in

Science and Government   21

applied science during the war,[11] succeeded to the job of permanent secretary, that is, the chief official responsible to a minister. Such chief officials in England have greater power, and more influence in determining policy, than their opposite numbers in the United States. In England they are right at the heart of the Establishment, and in a good many ways are more steadily and continuously important than their political bosses. Tizard fitted into that world from the start. He was not exactly an administrator's administrator, but he was liked and trusted by the high officials. They were in origin and in general attitude, if we forget his streak of scientific radicalism, very much like himself. He liked Whitehall. He liked the corridors of power. He liked the Athenaeum. He liked his colleagues, men like himself devoted, upright, and tough, though nothing like so outspoken as he was. When he moved off to become rector of the Imperial College, London, in 1929, he did not leave this inner English official world.

During those same years, Lindemann was making his way in quite a different English world—the world of high society and conservative politics, which at the time, when "Society" had a practical function that is now obsolescent or dead, still overlapped. It may seem odd that it was so easy for someone without any social connections, who was not even English by birth, who

22 Science and Government

was about as little like a typical specimen of the English upper classes as one can comfortably imagine, to penetrate right into the inner sanctums. But it is really very simple. It is only a puzzle if one approaches English society with Proustian illusions. Lindemann was rich: he was also determined. For generations English society has been wide open to, defenceless against, rich and determined men. The more so if they happen to be intelligent. So within a matter of months rather than years Lindemann was eating his singular vegetarian meals at a good many of the great English houses. He became known among smart people, with somewhat unfortunate infantilism, as "the Prof." He was very soon an intimate of Lord Birkenhead (F. E. Smith), and through Birkenhead he met Winston Churchill and began, apparently almost at first sight, a friendship which determined the rest of his life.

This friendship was utterly loyal on both sides, and continued so until Lindemann's death. A good deal of Lindemann's social progress was snobbish, an escape from inner defeats. But his devotion to Churchill was the purest thing in his life. It was quite unaffected, or perhaps more strengthened than weakened, by Churchill's ten years out of office (1929–1939) when it looked as though he were one of a hundred great men *manqués*, one of those with a brilliant future behind them. Churchill's loyalty to Lindemann was

Science and Government 23

also absolute. Later on, Lindemann, as Churchill knew well enough, became a cause of friction with Churchill's other intimates, something of a political liability. Churchill didn't budge an inch.

Why this friendship? a good many people have asked. They appeared a pretty incompatible pair. Churchill does not seem at first glance the obvious soulmate for a fanatical ascetic, a teetotal nonsmoking vegetarian. But the question, like a similar question about Roosevelt and Harry Hopkins, is without meaning unless one knew both men, not just well, but as well as they knew each other. Why any friendship, as far as that goes?[12]

VI.

In 1934 both Tizard and Lindemann were nearly fifty. Of the two, Tizard had been by a long way the more successful, though even he, judged by the standard he set himself, had not lived up to his promise. He was a trusted man of affairs, he had been knighted, he was head of a university institution, but in his own eyes he had not done much.

As for Lindemann, he had done much less. The professional physicists did not take him seriously as a

24   Science and Government

scientist, and dismissed him as a cranky society pet. Scientifically his name was worth little. He was the intimate friend of a politician whose name was scarcely worth as much.

Then, quite suddenly, Tizard was given the chance for which he was made. England was strategically in a desperately vulnerable position, for reasons—the tiny size of the country, the density of the population—which apply more harshly today. In 1934 Baldwin was the main figure in the government, and it was only two years since he had said lugubriously: "The bomber will always get through."

In public, rebellious politicians like Churchill were attacking the whole of the government's defence policy. In secret, the government scientists, the military staffs, the high officials, were beating round for some sort of defence. There was nothing accidental about this. It was predictable that England, more vulnerable to air attack than any major country, would spend more effort trying to keep bombers off. But there was something accidental and unpredictable in Tizard being given his head.

The Air Ministry, under the influence of their scientific adviser, H. E. Wimperis, himself prodded by a bright young government scientist called A. P. Rowe,[13] set up a Committee for the Scientific Study of Air Defence. Its terms of reference were as flat as usual: "To

Science and Government   25

consider how far advances in scientific and technical knowledge can be used to strengthen the present methods of defence against hostile aircraft." The committee was nothing very important to start with. No one took much notice when its membership was announced. There may have been slight curiosity about the appointment, which was entirely due to Wimperis,[14] of Tizard as chairman. The appointment would not and could not have happened, though, if Tizard had not been so well connected in official life.

Well, that committee was called the Tizard Committee almost from its first meeting. It is slightly touching that in his diary Tizard, who could not use that title, never seems to have been quite certain what its official title really was.

From the first meeting on January 28th, 1935 he gripped the problems. This was the job for which he was born. Quite soon, by the summer of that year, small ripples of confidence oozed under the secret doors and penetrated Whitehall, almost the only ripples of confidence that touched the official world during those years. Tizard insisted on a very small committee which he chose himself. Wimperis had to be there, Rowe was brought in as secretary, but at the beginning there were only two members of independent standing, A. V. Hill and P. M. S. Blackett. Both of these were eminent scientists, of a quite different

26 *Science and Government*

order of accomplishment from Tizard or Lindemann. Hill was one of the most distinguished physiologists in the world and had won a Nobel prize in 1922. Blackett, who was only thirty-seven at this time, was one of Rutherford's most brilliant pupils, and later himself won a Nobel prize.[15]

I doubt if their scientific stature was Tizard's first reason for choosing them. He was an exceptionally good picker of men. Like all good pickers, he was not distracted by much; he was thinking of what the men could do. It did not matter to him that Hill was a very unorthodox conservative, hotly out of sympathy with the Baldwin-Chamberlain policy, the policy of Tizard's own Establishment friends. It did not matter to him—as it would certainly have done to more cowardly men—that Blackett was a radical, the most distinguished figure among all the radical young scientists, who were bitterly antifascist and who distrusted every move that our own government made. I can say that without hedging, because I was one of them myself.

Tizard did not care. He knew that Hill and Blackett were men who were equipped not only with technical insight, but with strong characters and capacity for decision. That was what he wanted. There was not much time to play with. And I have, though I can produce no evidence for it, a strong feeling that he wanted just one other thing. He wanted the members

Science and Government   27

of his committee to have a natural sympathy for and identification with military men. Hill had been successful in the Army in the first world war, and had edited a classical work on antiaircraft gunnery. Blackett, before he turned to physics, had been a professional naval officer.

That was a factor in their success, I am convinced. Because the first task was not only a scientific choice, which they made quickly, but also an effort of indoctrination in the services (and a mutual give and take between serving officers and scientists) without which the choice was useless. The choice itself faced them like an "either/or." *Either* what was later called by its American name of radar, but in these aboriginal days was known as R.D.F., was the device to back: *or* there was nothing to back.

The committee made up its mind about that before the device really existed. Watson Watt, who was the pioneer of radar in England, working in the Radio Research Laboratory of the D.S.I.R., had done some preliminary experiments. This device might, not certainly but possibly, work in real war in three or four years. Nothing else possibly could. Tizard, Hill, Blackett had faith in their own reasoning. Without fuss, and without backward glances, the choice was made. That was only a resolution on paper, and they had to make it actual.

28   *Science and Government*

The administrative mechanism by which this was done is itself interesting. In form the Air Minister, Lord Swinton,[16] arranged for a new high-level committee which was to act as a subcommittee of the Committee of Imperial Defence. Over this new body he himself presided, and on to it was brought the government's chief military critic, Winston Churchill. In fact, however, one has got to imagine a great deal of that apparently casual to-ing and fro-ing by which high English business gets done. As soon as the Tizard committee thought there was something in radar, one can take it that Tizard would lunch with Hankey[17] at the Athenaeum; Hankey, the secretary of the Cabinet, would find it convenient to have a cup of tea with Swinton and Baldwin. If the Establishment had not trusted Tizard as one of their own, there might have been a waste of months or years. In fact, everything went through with the smoothness, the lack of friction, and the effortless speed which can only happen in England when the Establishment is behind one. Within a very short time the Tizard Committee were asking for millions of pounds, and getting it without a blink of an eye. Two successive secretaries of the Cabinet, Hankey and Bridges,[18] did much more than their official duty in pushing the project through.

The second active job was, in particular, to persuade the serving officers of the Air Staff that radar was their

Science and Government   29

one hope and, in general, to make scientists and military people understand each other. Here again this might have been impossible. In fact, with the exception of those concerned with bombing policy, the senior officers were ready to be convinced as soon as Tizard started to talk.[19] They often thought of putting him in uniform: but that would have defeated his whole virtue as an interpreter between the two sides. "I utterly refuse to wear a busby," he used to say. Fairly soon he had not only got radar stations in principle accepted and hoped for, but also succeeded, with the help of Blackett's exceptional drive and insight, in beginning to teach one lesson each to the scientists and the military, lessons that Tizard and Blackett went on teaching for twenty years.

The lesson to the military was that you cannot run wars on gusts of emotion. You have to think scientifically about your own operations. This was the start of operational research,[20] the development of which was Blackett's major personal feat in the 1939–45 war.[21] The lesson to the scientists was that the prerequisite of sound military advice is that the giver must convince himself that, if he were responsible for action, he would himself act so. It is a difficult lesson to learn. If it were learnt, the number of theoretical treatises on the future of war would be drastically reduced.

The committee met for the first time, as I said, in

30 *Science and Government*

January 1935. By the end of 1935 its important decisions were in effect taken. By the end of 1936 most of those decisions were translated into action. It was one of the most effective small committees in history. But before it clinched its choices, there was a most picturesque row.

The committee had been set up, as we saw, from inside the Air Ministry. One of the reasons was, no doubt, to forestall criticism from outside, which came most loudly and effectively from Churchill. In 1934 he had publicly challenged the government's underestimate of the size of Hitler's air force. His figures, which had been produced by Lindemann, were much nearer the truth than the government's. Thus, simultaneously, there were going on the secret deliberations and discussions of the Tizard Committee, and an acrimonious military argument in full light in the House of Commons and the press, with Churchill the antigovernment spokesman.

It is one of the classical cases of "closed" politics coexisting with "open" politics. Passing from one to the other, an observer would not have known that he was dealing with the same set of facts. By the middle of 1935 Baldwin, who had just in form as well as fact become Prime Minister, wanted to reduce the temperature of the "open" military argument. He used the orthodox manoeuvre of asking Churchill in. Not into

Science and Government   31

the Cabinet: the personal rifts were too deep for that, but onto the new Swinton Committee, the *political* committee to which I have just referred, which was to keep a supervisory eye on air defence.

The history is very tangled at this point. No minutes have ever been published, but if I know Hankey and his colleagues at all—and I had the good luck to work under them a short time later—I have not much doubt that on the one hand they felt confident that they could give the Tizard Committee its head (Tizard sat himself on the political committee and made his requests for money to it), and that on the other hand it could not do harm, and might do good, if Churchill were given exact information of what was actually being done, rather than inexact.

Roughly that was what happened, but there were other consequences. Churchill entered the political committee, retaining the right to criticise in public and insisting that Lindemann, as his personal scientific adviser, be given a place on the Tizard Committee. Both these conditions were reasonable enough: but then the private war began.

Almost from the moment that Lindemann took his seat in the committee room, the meetings did not know half an hour's harmony or work undisturbed. I must say, as one with a taste for certain aspects of human behaviour, I should have dearly liked to be

32   *Science and Government*

there. The faces themselves would have been a nice picture. Lindemann, Hill, and Blackett were all very tall men of distinguished physical presence—Blackett sculptured and handsome, Hill ruddy and English, Lindemann pallid, heavy, Central European. Blackett and Hill would be dressed casually, like academics. Tizard and Lindemann, who were both conventional in such things, would be wearing black coats and striped trousers, and both would come to the meetings in bowler hats. At the table Blackett and Hill, neither of them specially patient men nor overfond of listening to nonsense, sat with incredulity through diatribes by Lindemann, scornful, contemptuous, barely audible, directed against any decision that Tizard had made, was making, or ever would make. Tizard sat it out for some time. He could be irritable, but he had great resources of temperament, and he knew that this was too serious a time to let the irritability flash. He also knew, from the first speech that Lindemann made in committee, that the friendship of years was smashed.

There must have been hidden resentments and rancours, which we are now never likely to know and which had been latent long before this. No doubt Lindemann, who was a passionate man, with the canalised passion of the repressed, felt that he ought to have been doing Tizard's job. No doubt he felt, because no one ever had more absolute belief in his own

Science and Government   33

conclusions, that he would have done Tizard's job much better, and that his specifics for air defence were the right ones, and the only right ones. No doubt he felt, with his fanatical patriotism, that Tizard and his accomplices, these Blacketts, these Hills, were a menace to the country and ought to be swept away.

It may have been—there are some who were close to these events who have told me so—that all his judgments at these meetings were due to his hatred of Tizard, which had burst out as uncontrollably as love. That is, whatever Tizard wanted and supported, Lindemann would have felt unshakably was certain to be wrong and would have opposed. The other view is that Lindemann's scientific, as well as his emotional, temperament came in: it was not only hatred for Tizard, it was also his habit of getting self-blindingly attached to his own gadgety ideas that led him on. Whatever the motive was, he kept making his case to the committee in his own characteristic tone of grinding certainty. It was an unjustifiable case.

The issue in principle was very simple. Radar was not yet proved to work: but Tizard and the others, as I have said, were certain that it was the only hope. None of them was committed to any special gadget. That was not the cast of their minds. There was only a limited amount of time, of people, of resources. Therefore the first priority must be given to radar—

34   Science and Government

not only to making the equipment, but to making arrangements, well in advance even of the first tests, for its operational use. (It was in fact in the operational use of radar, rather than in the equipment, that England got a slight tactical lead.)

Lindemann would not have any of this. Radar was not proved. He demanded that it should be put much lower on the priority list and research on other devices given the highest priority. He had two pet devices of his own. One was the use of infra-red detection. This seemed wildly impracticable then, to any of the others and to anyone who heard the idea. It seems even more wildly impracticable now. The other putative device was the dropping, in front of hostile aircraft, of parachute bombs and parachute mines. Mines in various forms had a singular fascination for Lindemann. You will find Rube Goldberg-like inspirations about them— aerial mines, fluvial mines, and so on—all over the Churchillian minutes from 1939–1942.[22] They keep coming in as a final irritation to a hard-pressed man in Tizard's records of his conversations with Churchill. All these mine inspirations originated from Lindemann. None of them was ever any practical good at all.

For twelve months Lindemann ground on with his feud on the committee. He was tireless. He was ready at each meeting to begin again from the beginning. He

Science and Government   35

was quite unsoftened, quite impregnable to doubt. Only a very unusual man, and one of abnormal emotional resistance and energy, could sit with men so able and not be affected in the slightest regard.

They themselves were not affected so far as choice was concerned. Tizard went ahead with the radar decisions and they let Lindemann register his disagreement. But gradually they got worn down. Neither Blackett nor Hill was phlegmatic enough to endure this monomaniac tension for ever. In July 1936,[23] when the committee were preparing a report, Lindemann abused Tizard in his usual form, over the invariable issue of too much priority for radar, but in terms so savage that the secretaries had to be sent out of the room.[24]

At that point Blackett and Hill had had enough of it. They resigned and did not try to give an emollient excuse for doing so. Whether this was done after discussion with Tizard is not clear. No discussion was really necessary. They all believed that this friction was doing too much harm. They were all experienced enough to know that, with Churchill still out of office, they could make their own terms.

Within a short time the committee was reappointed. Tizard was still chairman, Blackett and Hill were still members. Lindemann, however, was not. He was replaced by E. V. Appleton, the greatest living

36   Science and Government

English expert on the propagation of radio waves. Radar itself was an application of Appleton's fundamental work. The announcement of his name meant, in the taciturn eloquence of official statements, a clear victory for radar and for Tizard. The radar stations and the radar organisation were ready, not perfect but working, in time for the Battle of Britain. This had a major, and perhaps a decisive, effect.

This cautionary story of the first Lindemann-Tizard collision seems to me to contain a number of lessons, some of them not obvious. But there is one, at the same time so obvious and so ironic that I shall mention it now. It is simply that the results of closed politics can run precisely contrary to the results of open politics. That is an occupational feature of the way in which closed politics works and the way in which secret choices are made. Probably not more than a hundred people had any information whatever about Tizard's first radar decision; not more than twenty people took any effective part in it, and at the point of choice not more than five or six.

While that was going on, so also was violent open politics, the open politics of the thirties, the most ferocious and deeply felt open politics of my lifetime. Nearly everyone I knew of my own age who was politically committed, that is, who had decided that fascism had at all costs to be stopped, wanted Churchill

Science and Government   37

brought into the government. Partly for his own gifts, partly as a symbol of a country which was not going to let the Nazis win by default. We signed collective letters about Churchill; we used what influence we had, which in those years was not much. We wanted a government which would resist, the kind of government we finally got in 1940. That was the position, I think, of Blackett and most of my liberal friends. It was certainly my own. Looking back, I think we were right, and if put back in those years again I should do what I did then.

The ifs of history are not very profitable—but if Churchill had been brought back to office, if open politics had gone the way my friends and I clamoured and implored that it should? We should, without any question, have been morally better prepared for war when it came. We should have been better prepared in the amount of war material. But, studying the story I have just told, I find it hard to resist the possibility that, in some essential technical respects, we might have been worse prepared. If Churchill had come into office, Lindemann would have come with him, as happened later. It is then very hard to imagine Lindemann not getting charge of the Tizard Committee. As I have said, I take a pretty Tolstoyan view of history in the large. In a broad sense I cannot easily accept that these small personal accidents could affect major destinies.

38   *Science and Government*

And yet . . . without getting the radar in time we should not have stood a good chance in the war that finally arrived. With Lindemann instead of Tizard, it seems at least likely that different technical choices would have been made. If that had been so, I still cannot for the life of me see how the radar system would have been ready in time.

These retrospective fears are not profitable. But I do not know of a clearer case where open and closed politics appear to tell such different stories and point to such different fates.

VII. wwwwwwwwwwww

The first round in the Tizard-Lindemann duel thus went to Tizard. When war came, he had got his air defence system working. He himself became scientific adviser to the Air Ministry, and his diary between September 1939 and May 1940 is quick, hurried, and lively, written at night after visits to airfields, on the job that he did better than anyone in any country, getting scientific methods into the heads of the young officers, infusing them with his own enthusiasm and his own sense of scientific fact.

Things were going pretty well scientifically that

Science and Government 39

winter, but he had another preoccupation. He had arranged for A. V. Hill to be sent on a mission to Washington, and both of them had become convinced that there were overwhelming arguments for telling the American scientists the whole of our radar and other military scientific secrets. Nearly all the English scientists agreed—Cockcroft, Oliphant, Blackett all pressed the matter. Nearly everyone else disagreed.[25] The written record is simultaneously comic and dreary, with just the kind of comic dreariness one always meets when people get seized by the euphoria of secrecy. Various nodding heads said that United States security could in no circumstances be trusted. Various others, including some who should have known better, thought the United States had nothing to offer.

Tizard became distinctly irascible, but otherwise was getting a good deal of his own way. Churchill had become First Lord of the Admiralty as soon as war broke out, and Lindemann was in Whitehall as his personal adviser. But for the moment there was an uneasy balance of power; Lindemann could not touch the air arrangements. From the papers it looks as though Tizard was as happy and as occupied in those months as at any time in his public life.

Then came May 10th, the German attack on France, Churchill in power. Tizard knew the military dangers as well as anyone alive. He also probably knew

40   *Science and Government*

that his own days of authority would not last long. If so, his diary entries for that day and May 11th are among the masterpieces of English phlegm.

Friday, May 10. Left Oxford 9 a.m. for Farnborough by air. Saw de Burgh and discussed with him experimental work on A. I. In particular some work on frequency modulation. R. A. E. have made progress in aerial design to eliminate some of the effects of ground reflection, and Mitchell is optimistic: too much so, I think. No clear evidence that method of frequency modulation is better than the pulse method.

Saturday, May 11. From Hill Head to Tangmere. Discussed flying trials of A. I. Was told that ordinary C. H. interception was so bad that there was little hope of getting good A. I. interception by night until day interception was improved. I told them that I thought it better to concentrate on day interception with the help of A. I. rather than do night interceptions now.[26]

The German armies cut through France. Churchill and Lindemann were in 10 Downing Street, getting ready to take control of the war, including the scientific war. Tizard's diary goes on just like those two extracts, full of his actions, advice, memoranda. Of course, there is a great inertia behind anyone living the active life. It is a characteristic of a man of action, and Tizard was very much a man of action, that he goes on with his activity until he is stopped.

Science and Government   41

He was soon stopped. He was stopped in a somewhat peculiar fashion. On June 4 he was summoned to see Lindemann at 10 Downing Street. Maddeningly, there is no record of the conversation; I doubt if anything very direct was said on either side. The diary simply reports: "June 4. Thence to see Lindemann at 10 Downing Street. Apparently he had been told by the P. M. to 'drive ahead' with anything new that may be of use this summer, and there is enough overlapping of responsibility to hinder almost anything useful being done."[27]

Tizard must have known that he was out. But the particular way in which he was shown to be out may have come as a surprise. On June 7 he attended a meeting of his own Ministry, of which he was still the official scientific adviser—with his own Minister in the Chair. The air marshals and permanent officials were there. So was Lindemann. And it was Lindemann who laid down what the scientific programme should be. Tizard wrote that night: "Doubtful whether S. of S. really expected me. I tried to keep them straight about use of A. I. and G. L. for searchlights—but do not know if I succeeded. I left before the meeting was over as it did not appear that good could be done by staying."[28]

In the next few days Tizard went on with his work and at times saw his friends. A good many of them

42 *Science and Government*

seem to have thought that a man who had already been proved right so often could not be got rid of so contemptuously.

Friday, June 21. Meeting at 10 Downing Street to consider enemy methods of navigation. P. M. in chair—present Lindemann, S. of S., C. A. S., C. in C's Bomber and Fighter Command, Watson Watt, R. V. Jones and myself. Various decisions reached but would have been reached without those commotions in ordinary way. Afternoon meeting presided over by S. of S. to discuss progress on new developments. As unsatisfactory as previous meeting. Afterwards went to Athenaeum and wrote letter definitely resigning. Showed it to C. A. S. who agreed it was inevitable and asked me to suggest a post of authority for myself. Said this was better left for two or three weeks.[29]

The Chief of Air Staff, Sir Cyril Newell, was, like most of the military people, a devoted supporter of Tizard's. But when they talked of a post of authority, even Tizard, usually clear-sighted, was deluding himself. He was to perform one more first-rate service that year: he was to take part in the classical scientific-military quarrel in 1942; but, in the sense he had known it, there was to be no more authority for him in that war.

In a few weeks they had thought up something for him to do. Someone, possibly to tempt or mollify him, had revived his old idea of scientific exchange with the United States.

Science and Government   43

July 30. A meeting with Fairey in the hall of M. A. P.
He said, "I am going to be a member of your staff." I
said, "What staff?" He replied that Beaverbrook had just
told him that I was to lead a mission to America and that
he, Fairey, was to be a member. As Beaverbrook could not
see me, Rowlands, the Permanent Secretary of M. A. P.,
took me to his room and explained that the P. M. wanted
me to lead a mission to America for the exchange of
technical information . . . I was given a provisional list of
"secrets" I could impart, and of information I was to ask
for. I said I certainly would not go unless I was given a
free hand . . . It looked to me at first sight as rather a neat
method of getting a troublesome person out of the way
for a time![30]

That was, of course, at least part of the truth. If
Tizard had been playing politics he would not have
gone. In times of crisis, as all kinds of men have found
out, from Trotsky downwards, the first mistake is to
absent oneself. But Tizard had always believed in what
such a mission could do.

August 1. Called on Prime Minister at 5.45. Had to
wait some time as the Archbishop was with him, which, as
the private secretary explained, had quite thrown out the
timetable. The P. M. quite emphatic that the mission was
important and that he particularly wanted me to lead it.
I asked if he would give me a free hand and would rely
on my discretion. He said "of course"—and would I write
down exactly what I wanted. So I said I would go, and

44 *Science and Government*

went into the lobby and wrote out a paper which I left with his secretary. Then I rang up Rowlands and told him that I had accepted and that the P. M. was going to give me full discretion. He said that was quite different from what the P. M. had previously said![31]

Flying the Atlantic in August 1940 meant that a man put his affairs in order. Before he left Tizard arranged that, in case of accidents, his war-time diaries should go to the Royal Society. Those are the diaries from which I have been quoting. He had a proper pride in what he had achieved, and a proper rancour for the way he had been treated. He did not doubt that, if and when competent persons studied the evidence—the diaries and notebooks are full of scientific arguments from 1935 to 1939, which it would not be suitable to quote here—he would get his due.

But no accidents happened, and the mission, on which John Cockcroft was his second in command, was one of the successes of both their lives. American scientists, both at the time and since, have spoken, with extreme generosity, of the effect that visit made. It is true that, mainly because the English had been forced to think in order to survive at all, in most military scientific fields they were ahead. This was pre-eminently true of radar. Although English, American, and German scientists had all begun developing radar

Science and Government 45

at about the same time—which incidentally tells one something of the nature of "secret" discoveries—by 1940 the English had carried it further.

Tizard and Cockcroft carried with them a black leather suitcase which Miss Geary, Tizard's secretary, was forced to keep under her bed. She did not know it contained nearly all the important new English war devices—and, of a different order of importance from the rest, the new cavity magnetron. Mr. James Phinney Baxter, writing the story of the American scientific war, has called the black box "the most valuable cargo ever brought to our shores" and "the single most important item in reverse lease-lend." The magnetron, which was invented by Randall and Boot in Oliphant's laboratory at Birmingham, was probably the most valuable single device in the Hitler war.[32] The sight of it set American scientists working all out sixteen months before the United States was in the war at all. As Blackett has said:

This imaginative act of trust, which Tizard and A. V. Hill first envisaged and finally forced through Whitehall, had immensely beneficial effects on the scientific aspects of the allied war effort. Cockcroft reminds us that the mission was magnificently organised by Tizard, and that he had the inspiration to bring a mixed team of serving officers and scientists. For the first time our American

46   Science and Government

friends heard civilian scientists discussing authoritatively the instruments of war, and then heard the Service people following on with practical experience.[33]

When he returned from the mission, Tizard found that he was still out. There was no real job for him. He worked, as a kind of free-lance scientific adviser, in the Ministry of Aircraft Production. Then the R. A. F., which had throughout been loyal to him, put him on the Air Council. But neither of those posts made anything like a full call on his powers. In fact, no post could, while Lindemann was making all the major scientific decisions on the English side of the war.

I saw something of Tizard at the time. He was a very high-spirited man, too high-spirited to be bitter. He was also remarkably free from self-pity. He got a lot of fun out of the solemn paraphernalia of English official life. The dinners at City Companies, the various Boards of Governors of which he was a member —to most of us all that would not have been much consolation, but it was to him. Still, he was only 56, he was at the height of his abilities, he was chafing at the leash. I think he welcomed the final row with Lindemann, not only because he was certain he was right, but also because it gave him something to do.

Science and Government   47

~~~~~~~~~~~~~~~~ VIII.

The row occurred in 1942, and it occurred over strategic bombing. We have got to remember that it was very hard for the Western countries to make any significant military effort in Europe that year. The great battles were taking place on the Russian land. So it was natural, and good military sense, that the Western leaders were receptive to any idea for action. It is also true—and this was not such good military sense—that the English and Americans had, for years past, believed in strategic bombing as no other countries had. Countries which had thought deeply about war, like Germany and Russia, had no faith in strategic bombing and had not invested much productive capacity or many élite troops in it. The English had, years before the war began. The strategy had not been thought out. It was just an unrationalised article of faith that strategic bombing was likely to be our most decisive method of making war. I think it is fair to say that Lindemann had always believed in this faith with characteristic intensity.

Early in 1942 he was determined to put it into action. By this time he was Lord Cherwell and a member of the Cabinet, and he produced a cabinet paper

48   *Science and Government*

on the strategic bombing of Germany. Some cabinet
papers are restricted to members of the Cabinet only,
and Lindemann occasionally used this technique for
circulating a scientific proposal; since he was the only
scientist in the Cabinet, discussion was reduced to a
minimum. But the paper on bombing went out to the
top government scientists.

It described, in quantitative terms, the effect on
Germany of a British bombing offensive in the next
eighteen months (approximately March 1942—September 1943). The paper laid down a strategic policy.
The bombing must be directed essentially against German working-class houses. Middle-class houses have
too much space round them, and so are bound to waste
bombs; factories and "military objectives" had long
since been forgotten, except in official bulletins, since
they were much too difficult to find and hit. The paper
claimed that—given a total concentration of effort on
the production and use of bombing aircraft—it would
be possible, in all the larger towns of Germany (that
is, those with more than 50,000 inhabitants), to de-
stroy 50 per cent of all houses.

Let me break off for a minute. It is possible, I suppose, that some time in the future people living in a
more benevolent age than ours may turn over the official records and notice that men like us, men well-edu-
cated by the standards of the day, men fairly kindly by

Science and Government   49

the standards of the day, and often possessed of strong human feelings, made the kind of calculation I have just been describing. Such calculations, on a much larger scale, are going on at this moment in the most advanced societies we know. What will people of the future think of us? Will they say, as Roger Williams said of some of the Massachusetts Indians, that we were wolves with the minds of men? Will they think that we resigned our humanity? They will have the right.

At the time I heard some talk of the famous cabinet paper. I have to say this about my own attitude and that of the people I knew best. We had never had the conventional English faith in strategic bombing, partly on military and partly on human grounds. But now it came to the point it was not Lindemann's ruthlessness that worried us most,[34] it was his calculations.

The paper went to Tizard. He studied the statistics. He came to the conclusion, quite impregnably, that Lindemann's estimate of the number of houses that could possibly be destroyed was five times too high.

The paper went to Blackett. Independently he studied the statistics. He came to the conclusion, also quite impregnably, that Lindemann's estimate was six times too high.

Everyone agreed that, if the amount of possible destruction was as low as that calculated by Tizard and

50   *Science and Government*

Blackett, the bombing offensive was not worth concentrating on. We should have to find a different strategy, both for production and for the use of élite troops. It fell to Tizard to argue this case, to put forward the view that the bombing strategy would not work.

I do not think that, in secret politics, I have ever seen a minority view so unpopular. Bombing had become a matter of faith. I sometimes used to wonder whether my administrative colleagues, who were clever and detached and normally the least likely group of men to be swept away by any faith, would have acquiesced in this one, as on the whole they did, if they had had even an elementary knowledge of statistics. In private we made the bitter jokes of a losing side. "There are the Fermi-Dirac statistics," we said. "The Einstein-Bose statistics. And the new Cherwell nonquantitative statistics." And we told stories of a man who added up two and two and made four. "He is not to be trusted," the Air Ministry then said. "He has been talking to Tizard and Blackett."

The Air Ministry fell in behind the Lindemann paper. The minority view was not only defeated, but squashed. The atmosphere was more hysterical than is usual in English official life; it had the faint but just perceptible smell of a witch hunt. Tizard was actually called a defeatist. Strategic bombing, according

Science and Government   51

to the Lindemann policy, was put into action with
every effort the country could make.

The ultimate result is well known. Tizard had calculated that Lindemann's estimate was five times too
high. Blackett had put it at six times too high. The
bombing survey after the war revealed that it had been
ten times too high.

After the war Tizard only once said "I told you
so." He gave just one lecture on the theory and practice of aerial bombing. "No one thinks now that it
would have been possible to defeat Germany by bombing alone. The actual effort in manpower and resources
that was expended on bombing Germany was greater
than the value in manpower of the damage caused."

During the war, however, after he had lost that second conflict with Lindemann, he went through a pain-
ful time. It was not easy, for a man as tough and brave
as men are made, and a good deal prouder than most
of us, to be called a defeatist. It was even less easy to be
shut out of scientific deliberations, or to be invited to
them on condition that he did not volunteer an opinion unless asked. It is astonishing in retrospect that
he should have been offered such humiliations. I do
not think that there has been a comparable example
in England this century.

However, the Establishment in England has a

52 *Science and Government*

knack of looking after its own. At the end of 1942 he was elected to the presidency of Magdalen College, Oxford. This is a very honourable position, which most official Englishmen would accept with gratitude. So did Tizard. There are no continuous diary entries at this period, although now he had plenty of time. For once his vitality seems to have flagged.

I think there is little doubt that, sitting in the Lodgings at Magdalen during the last thirty months of war, he often thought of Whitehall with feelings both of outrage and regret. Here he was, in one of the most splendid of honorific jobs, but his powers were rusting —powers that were uniquely fitted for this war. He knew, more accurately than most men, what he was capable of. He believed, both in his dignified exile in Oxford and to the end of his life, that if he had been granted a fair share of the scientific direction between 1940 and 1943, the war might have ended a bit earlier and with less cost. As one goes over the evidence it is hard not to agree with him.

After the war, he and Lindemann were never reconciled. In Whitehall they performed a Box and Cox act which had a note of sarcastic comedy. In 1945, with the political defeat of Churchill, Lindemann went back to his professorial chair at Oxford. Tizard was promptly invited by the Labour Government to become chairman of the Advisory Council on Scientific

Science and Government   53

Policy, and also of the Defence Research Policy Committee, that is, to become the government's chief scientific adviser, very much in the mode that Killian and Kistiakowsky have been employed in the United States. In 1951 Churchill and Lindemann returned to power. Tizard rapidly resigned.

It caused a good deal of comment that Tizard was never put in the House of Lords, but that did not trouble him. The only thing he was known to grumble about was his pension, which, as I previously mentioned, was derisory. In his very last years, when he and Lindemann were both getting old, he had to take some directorships to make money for himself and provide for his wife. Lindemann died in 1957. Tizard outlived him by two years.

IX.

There ends my cautionary story. Now I want to suggest just which cautions we can reasonably extract from it. First we have got to allow for those features of English government and administration which are peculiar to us. There are some features which do not travel, which are inexplicable and boring to Americans and Russians involved in their own problems of

54 Science and Government

science and government. These features are, as American publishers used to say in pained tones of English novels, too British. The chief of them, I think, is the small size, the tightness, the extreme homogeneity, of the English official world. I. I. Rabi once told me that, on his first visit to England in wartime, I believe in 1942, he found Churchill actually handling the prototype of a new radar set in No. 10 Downing Street. Rabi wondered, why did the English insist on running the war as though it were a very small family business?

It is perfectly true that the English unconsciously adopt all sorts of devices for making their population, genuinely small by world standards, seem a good deal smaller than it really is: just as the United States, it seems to me, does exactly the reverse.

But, though that is true, I do not think it affects the major lessons of my story. There is a great deal in closed politics which is essentially the same in any country and in any system. If we are going to begin to understand what goes on, and so do better, I am sure it is wise to take for granted that other countries are much the same as ourselves, not vastly different. To a friendly observer, it often seems that Americans endanger themselves most when they get most possessed by a sense of their own uniqueness. In all the problems I am now discussing, government science, closed politics, secret choices, there is no such uniqueness.

Science and Government   55

In these matters, by the sheer nature of the operations, all countries have to follow very similar laws. No country's governmental science is any "freer" than any other's, nor are its secret scientific choices. I beg you to listen to this. It is said by someone who knows you a bit, who loves you a lot, and who is passionately anxious to see your generous creative forces set loose in the world. You have no special advantages in this domain of science and decision. Listening to American and Soviet scientists, trying to study the way in which you both do your government science, I am struck, not by the differences, but by the similarities. If there is any difference, it is perhaps that, because of the special privileges and autonomy of the Soviet Academy, Russian scientists take a slightly loftier attitude: and also, though this may be a superficial impression, I fancy their major choices involve more scientific minds, are slightly more broadly based, than with you or us.

So I believe we are in the same boat and that all countries can learn from each other's concrete experience. We all know the ideal solutions. First, you can abolish some, though probably not all, secret choices as soon as you abolish nation-states. Second, the special aura of difficulty and mystery about these choices will at least be minimised as soon as all politicians and administrators are scientifically educated, or at any

56   Science and Government

rate not scientifically illiterate. Neither of these ideal solutions is in sight. We may therefore not be entirely wasting our time if we try to analyse some phenomena of scientific choice in "closed" politics.

I have used the phrase "closed politics" before. I mean any kind of politics in which there is no appeal to a larger assembly—larger assembly in the sense of a group of opinion, or an electorate, or on an even bigger scale what we call loosely "social forces." For instance, some of the struggles in an English Cabinet partake of the nature of closed politics: but this is not pure closed politics, since the Prime Minister or any member can if pressed move from personal to mass opinion. On the other hand, almost all the secret scientific choices are something like pure closed politics.

In my type-specimen, during the whole of his conflicts with Lindemann, Tizard had no larger body of support to call on. If he had been able to submit the bombing controversy[35] to the Fellows of the Royal Society, or the general population of professional scientists, Lindemann would not have lasted a week. But of course Tizard could do no such thing: and that is true of most conflicts in government science and of all secret choices.

So we find ourselves looking at the classical situations of closed politics. The most obvious fact which hits you in the eye is that personalities and personal

Science and Government   57

relations carry a weight of responsibility which is out of proportion greater than any they carry in open politics. Despite appearances, we are much nearer than in ordinary government to personal power and personal choice. A crude result is that, at this moment, all countries are not unlikely to be at the mercy of scientific salesmen.

In the Tizard-Lindemann story, we saw three of the characteristic forms of closed politics. These three forms are not often completely separable, and usually fuse into each other, but they are perhaps worth defining. The first is committee politics. There is, of course, a complex morphology of committee politics, and everyone who has ever lived in any society, in a tennis club, a factory dramatic group, a college faculty, has witnessed some of its expressions. The archetype of all these is that kind of committee where each member speaks with his individual voice, depends upon his personality alone for his influence, and in the long run votes with an equal vote.

The Tizard Committee itself was a good example. The members did not represent anyone but themselves. Their only way of affecting conclusions was by their own mana and their own arguments. If it came to a disagreement, then the ultimate decision, which any official committee leans over backwards to avoid, was by means of "counting heads." That was what hap-

58   Science and Government

pened, though the circumstances were dramatic, when Lindemann was opposing Tizard over the priority for radar. Everyone round the table knew that it was three to one against Lindemann.[36] In this archetype of a committee, with personalities of approximately equal toughness, with no external recourse except a Churchill out of power and so possessing only nuisance value, that meant his case was lost.

I have just said that any official committee, certainly any English official committee, is reluctant about taking an open vote. I believe that such a vote has never in fact been taken in the English Cabinet: but of course the substance of a vote, the way opinion has divided, is obvious enough. If you want open votes, so as to see the committee operation in its full beauty, you need to go to societies which do not damp down the friction of personalities—such as the smaller colleges of my own Cambridge, which cheerfully proceed to open votes on all sorts of controversies, including personal appointments. I suppose the most famous open vote of this century happened when, in October 1917, smuggled for safety into the house of a political enemy, Lenin moved his resolution to the Central Committee of the Bolshevik party "That . . . [very long parenthesis defining the conditions] . . . the Bolsheviks do now seize power." The voting was ten to

Science and Government 59

two in favour, with Kameniev and Zinoviev voting against.

There is nothing, by the way, in committee politics which is specially connected with American or English parliamentary institutions. The Venetian oligarchy were great masters of committee work and carried out most of their government by its means. The Council of Ten (which usually sat as a body of seventeen) and the Heads of the Ten (who were an inner committee of three) made most of the executive decisions. I doubt if there is much that any of us could have taught them about committee politics. In a book of mine some years ago I wrote about a meeting of high officials:

These men were fairer, and most of them a great deal abler, than the average: but you heard the same ripples below the words, as when any group of men chose anyone for any job. Put your ear to those meetings and you heard the intricate, labyrinthine and unassuageable rapacity, even in the best of men, of the love of power. If you have heard it once—say, in electing the chairman of a tiny dramatic society, it does not matter where—you have heard it in colleges, in bishoprics, in ministries, in cabinets: men do not alter because the issues they decide are bigger scale.[37]

I should still stand by each word of that.

The second form of closed politics I think I had

60 Science and Government

better call "hierarchical politics"—the politics of a chain of command, of the services, of a bureaucracy, of a large industry. On the surface these politics seem very simple. Just get hold of the man at the top, and the order will go down the line. So long as you have collected the boss, you have got nothing else to worry about. That is what people believe—particularly people who are both cynical and unworldly, which is one of my least favourite combinations—who are not used to hierarchies. Nothing could be more naive.

Chain-of-command organisations do not work a bit like that. English organisations, our Civil Service, our armed Services, are moderately well disciplined, by existing standards. Certainly our serving officers do not show the same enthusiasm for publicising their point of view, especially when they cut across higher authority, as some American officers appear to show. But, in reality, though not on the surface, both our countries work much the same way.

To get anything done in any highly articulated organisation, you have got to carry people at all sorts of levels. It is their decisions, their acquiescence or enthusiasm (above all, the absence of their passive resistance), which are going to decide whether a strategy goes through in time. Everyone competent to judge agrees that this was how Tizard guided and shoved the radar strategy. He had the political and administrative

Science and Government　　61

bosses behind him from the start (Churchill and Lindemann being then ineffective). He had also the Air Staff and the Chiefs of Command. But he spent much effort on persuading and exhorting the junior officers who would have to control the radar chains when they were ready.

In the same way, he was persuading and exhorting the scientists who were designing the hardware, and the administrators who had to get it made. Like all men who understand institutions, Tizard was always asking himself the questions "Where to go to? For which job?" Often, for a real decision as opposed to a legalistic one, the chap who is going to matter is a long way down the line. Administrators like Hankey and Bridges were masters of this kind of institutional understanding, and they were able to prod and stroke, caress and jab, the relevant parts of the English organism, so that somehow or other, in a way that made organisational diagrams look very primitive, the radar chain got made.

I remember myself, very early in the war, being sent for by a high functionary, much to the bafflement and, I am afraid, to the irritation, of my official superiors. I was a junior official, having gone in as a temporary a few months before: but I had taken on myself the job of producing large numbers of radar scientists. As usual, everyone had forgotten the sheer human needs,

62   Science and Government

in terms of numbers of trained minds, of a new device. I got my summons and went off to the Treasury. My interlocutor was so many steps above me in the hierarchy that no regular communication was possible. That did not matter. Later on, we became friends. The interview, however, took about five minutes. Was this scheme going all right? Should we get enough men? At the right time? The answer to those questions was yes. Did I need any help? No, not just then. That was all. That is the way hierarchical politics sometimes has to work. Granted a serious objective, granted a long-term and unspoken respect for certain rules, it often works very well.

This is a form of politics which has not yet received the attention it needs, if one is going to have any feel, not for how an elaborate organisation is supposed to operate, but for how it does in fact.[38] It cuts across all kinds of romantic stereotypes of official power. The top bosses of great corporations like General Motors, or General Electric, or their English equivalents, could not act even if they wanted to, could not act by the intrinsic nature of their organisation, like the proprietors of a small film company. Blissful expressions of power, such as hire and fire, get more remote from reality the more elaborate your organisation is, and the nearer you are to the top of it. I suspect that hierarchical politics are probably more interesting and com-

Science and Government   63

plex in the United States than in any country in the world, certainly more interesting than in any country in the West.

The third form of politics in the Tizard-Lindemann story is the simplest. I shall call it "court politics." By court politics I mean attempts to exert power through a man who possesses a concentration of power. The Lindemann-Churchill relation is the purest example possible of court politics.

In 1940, as I described it, Lindemann asked Tizard to call on him at 10 Downing Street. At that time Tizard was the most senior scientific adviser in government employment. Lindemann had no official position whatever; he was the confidential friend of Churchill. Before the end of their conversation Tizard knew that his authority was over. Within three weeks he had resigned.

For another eighteen months, until the end of 1941, Lindemann still held no official position whatever: but he had more direct power than any scientist in history. Roosevelt had a court too, and there must have been a lot of court politics throughout his administrations; but, so far as I know, no scientist ever got near to being intimate with him, and Vannevar Bush and his colleagues were operating at the ordinary official distances and through the ordinary official techniques. Hitler had a court, but he, to an extent quite unparalleled,

64 *Science and Government*

kept the power to himself. Incidentally, no scientist seems to have got anywhere near him, though he was interested in weapons. His total lack of scientific comprehension was fortunate for the world.

Churchill and Lindemann, however, really did work together, on all scientific decisions and on a good many others, as one mind. In his early days as grey eminence to the Prime Minister, Lindemann made it obvious, by holding his interviews in 10 Downing Street or by threatening Churchill's intervention. Very soon this was not necessary. Bold men protested to Churchill about Lindemann's influence,[39] and were shown out of the room. Before long everyone in official England knew that the friendship was unbreakable, and that Lindemann held real power. Before long also men had accustomed themselves to that degree of power and jumped up behind it; for an overwhelming majority of men find a fascination in seeing power confidently used, and are hypnotised by it. Not entirely through self-seeking, though that enters too.

The fact that the bombing policy was forced through with so little opposition is a typical example of the hypnosis of power. A good many men read the Tizard and Blackett papers. A certain proportion felt, men being men, that, if a scientific statesman like Tizard could be ignominiously swept aside, lesser persons had

Science and Government   65

better keep quiet. It is very easy, in an atmosphere of crisis, in the midst of secret decisions, for men to surrender both their reason and their will. I can still hear someone, a man normally tough and intelligent, saying to me one black night: "The P. M. and Prof. have decided—and who are we to say them nay?"

Judged by the simple criterion of getting what he wanted, Lindemann was the most successful court politician of the age. One has to go back a long way, at least as far as Père Joseph, to find a grey eminence half as effective. Incidentally, there exists a romantic stereotype of the courtier—as someone supple, devoid of principle, thinking of nothing except keeping his place at court. Now Lindemann was, in functional terms, a supreme courtier; and yet no one could be more unlike that stereotype. Life is not as simple as that, nor as corrupt in quite that way. Throughout his partnership with Churchill, Lindemann remained his own man. A remarkable number of the ideas came from him. It was a two-sided friendship. There was admiration on Lindemann's side, of course, but so there was on Churchill's. It was a friendship of singular quality—certainly the most selfless and admirable thing in Lindemann's life, and in Churchill's, much richer in personal relations, it nevertheless ranked high. It is ironical that such a friendship, which had much

66   Science and Government

nobility and in private showed both men at their human best, should in public have led them into bad judgments.

In all closed politics the three forms I have isolated —committee politics, hierarchical politics, court politics—interweave, interact, and shift from one to the other.[40] That is independent of the objectives, which may be good or bad; it is simply the way men have to operate, in order to get anything done at all. I do not mean that as satire. *Satire is cheek.*[41] It is the revenge of those who cannot really comprehend the world or cope with it. No, I mean my description of politics to be taken as neutral statements. So far as I have been able to observe anything, this is how the world ticks— not only our world, but also the future world one can imagine, juster and more sensible than ours. It seems to me important that men of good will should make an effort to understand how the world ticks; it is the only way to make it tick better.

X.

After looking at the Tizard-Lindemann story, and reflecting a bit on the kinds of politics, can we find any guide to action? Is there any way, in this great un-

Science and Government   67

derground domain of science and government, in which we can arrange to make choices a little more reasonably?

Let me say at once that I have no easy answers at all. If there were any easy answers, they would have been found by now. The whole problem is an intractable one, one of the most intractable that organised society has thrown up. It is partly the expression, in political and administrative terms of the split between two cultures that I have said something about elsewhere.[42]

But, though the answers have not presented themselves, I think we have advanced far enough to know certain things to avoid. We know some of the sources of bad judgments and bad choices. I think most of us would agree that it is dangerous to have a solitary scientific overlord. It is specially dangerous to have him sitting in power, with no scientist near him, surrounded by politicians who think of him, as some of Churchill's colleagues thought of Lindemann, as the all-wise, all-knowing Prof. We have seen too much of that, and we should not like it to happen again.

And yet, as I say that, I wonder if I am becoming too cautious, too much in love with an old country's predilection for checks and balances. Lindemann made some bad choices, but he also drove some things through as a nonscientist could not have done. Im-

68   *Science and Government*

agine that, in that same position of solitary scientific power, Tizard had been installed: or that Vannevar Bush had been as close to Roosevelt as Lindemann was to Churchill. In either of those cases the positive good would have been startling. Still, I do not think it is overcautious to remember that that has never happened. The chances of getting a Tizard or a Bush as scientific overlord are pretty remote. On the whole, I am still inclined to believe that the obvious dangers outweigh the vestigial possibility of good.

That is fairly clear. We ought not to give any single scientist the powers of choice that Lindemann had. It is even clearer, in my mind at least, that there is a kind of scientist to whom we ought not to give any power of choice at all. We have seen some examples of how judgments were distorted, enough to specify some of the people to fight shy of. Various kinds of fear distort scientific judgments, just as they do other judgments: but, most of all, the self-deceiving factor seems to be a set of euphorias. The euphoria of gadgets; the euphoria of secrecy. They are usually, but not invariably, combined. They are the origin of 90 per cent of ill-judged scientific choices. Any scientist who is prone to these euphorias ought to be kept out of government decisions or choice-making, at almost any cost. It doesn't matter how good he is at his stuff. It

Science and Government 69

doesn't matter if the gadgets[43] are efficacious, like the atomic bomb, or silly, like Lindemann's parachute mines for dropping on airscrews.[44] It doesn't matter how confident he is; in fact, if he is confident because of the euphoria of gadgets, he is doubly dangerous.

The point is, anyone who is drunk with gadgets is a menace. Any choice he makes—particularly if it involves comparison with other countries—is much more likely to be wrong than right. The higher he climbs, the more he is going to mislead his own country.

The nearer he is to the physical presence of his own gadget, the worse his judgment is going to be. It is easy enough to understand. The gadget is *there*. It is one's own. One knows, no one can possibly know as well, all the bright ideas it contains, all the snags overcome. I have felt something like it at second hand, over gadgets I have seen developed. Seeing the first English jet flying in 1942, I could not believe this was not unique. It was like denying one's own identity to credit there was anything else like that in existence. As a matter of fact, of course, there were in existence quite a lot like that. The Germans had already got a jet flying even more impressively. In cold blood the probabilities dawn again, just as they dawned upon anyone connected with radar, who found the same

70   *Science and Government*

gadgets being developed in the same loving secrecy in England, in the United States, in Germany and elsewhere.

The overriding truth is a bleak one, if one is living in the physical presence of gadgets and spends one's creative force developing them: that societies at about the same level of technology will produce similar inventions. In military technology in particular, where the level of the United States and the U.S.S.R. is very much the same and where the investment of scientists and money is also similar, it would be astonishing if either society kept for long anything like a serious, much less a decisive, technical lead.

It is overwhelming odds that one country will get its nose in front in one field for a short time, the other somewhere else. This situation, fluctuating in detail but steady in the gross, is likely to continue without limit. It is quite unrealistic, and very dangerous, to imagine that the West as a whole can expect a permanent and decisive lead in military technology over the East as a whole. That expectation is a typical piece of gadgeteers' thinking. It has done the West more harm than any other kind of thinking. History and science do not work that way.

If one is not existing in the immediate presence of gadgets, it is a little less impossible to keep a kind of rudimentary common sense. The news of the first

Science and Government 71

atomic pile reached a few of us in England in 1943. In the somewhat inelegant language of the day, we knew the atomic bomb was on. We heard people, intoxicated by the discovery, predicting that it would give the United States unheard-of power for so long as one could foresee. We did not believe it. We had no special prescience, but we were outside the area of euphoria. We speculated on how long it would take a country with the scientific and technical capacity of Russia to catch up, once the discovery was known. We guessed about six years. We were wrong. One always overestimates these periods. It took them four.

It is one of the firmest convictions of most of the best administrators I have known that scientists, by and large, could not do their job. There are many reasons for this conviction, including various human frailties, and I shall return to it at the end. But there is one good one. Many administrators have had to listen to the advice of scientist-gadgeteers. To Bridges and his colleagues, to a good many of the high civil servants who played a part in the Tizard-Lindemann story, it must have appeared scarcely human that men should be so lacking in broad and detached judgment.[45] Most administrators would go on to feel that there is something of the gadgeteer hiding in every scientist.

I have to admit that there is something in it. I should phrase it rather differently. The gadgeteer's

72   Science and Government

temperament is an extreme example of a common scientific temperament. A great many scientists have a trace of the obsessional. Many kinds of creative science, perhaps most, one could not do without it. To be any good, in his youth at least, a scientist has to think of one thing, deeply and obsessively, for a long time. An administrator has to think of a great many things, widely, in their interconnections, for a short time. There is a sharp difference in the intellectual and moral temperaments. I believe, and I shall lay some stress on this later, that persons of scientific education can make excellent administrators and provide an element without which we shall be groping: but I agree that scientists in their creative periods do not easily get interested in administrative problems and are not likely to be much good at them.

The euphoria of secrecy goes to the head very much like the euphoria of gadgets. I have known men, prudent in other respects, who became drunk with it. It induces an unbalancing sense of power. It is not of consequence whether one is hugging to oneself a secret about one's own side or about the other. It is not uncommon to run across men, superficially commonplace and unextravagant, who are letting their judgment run wild because they are hoarding a secret about the other side—quite forgetting that someone

Science and Government 73

on the other side, almost indistinguishable from themselves, is hoarding a precisely similar secret about them. It takes a very strong head to keep secrets for years, and not go slightly mad. It isn't wise to be advised by anyone slightly mad.

XI.

I could go on accumulating negatives and empirical prescriptions. We know something about what not to do and whom not to pick. We can collect quite a few working tips from the Tizard-Lindemann story. For instance, the prime importance, in any crisis of action, of being positive what you want to do and of being able to explain it. It is not so relevant whether you are right or wrong. That is a second-order effect. But it is cardinal that you should be positive. In the radar struggle Tizard and his committee were positive that theirs was the only hope, and Lindemann had only quibbles and fragmentary ideas to set against it. Over bombing, Lindemann was positive that he had the recipe to win the war. Tizard was sure he was wrong, but had nothing so simple and unified to put in its place. Even at the highest level of decision, men do

74   *Science and Government*

not really relish the complexity of brute reality, and they will hare after a simple concept whenever one shows its head.

We also saw that a committee like the Tizard Committee is, in the right conditions, as sharp a tool for doing business as government can find. What are the conditions? As a sighting shot I should say:

(1) The objective must be clear and not too grandiloquently vast. A scientific committee set to advise on the welfare of all mankind is not likely to get very far. The objective of the Tizard Committee— to defend England in a foreseeable short-term future against air attack—is about as much as anyone can hope actually to cope with.

(2) The committee has got to be "placed" within the government structure. It is usually not difficult to do this, if one has people who know the government machine (or organism, since machine is a bad word) by touch. Different government machines need a different touch, and as a rule a foreigner, however well he knew the country, would dither about where the optimum place should be. To fit the local English structure, the Tizard Committee could not have been better placed, partly by good management, partly by good luck. It was not so high as to get out of touch with the working administrators and the serving officers, or to arouse too much envy (very important

Science and Government 75

in a compact country). But it had its own links with ministers and top civil servants. In the United States, if I have not got it wrong, there is not the same problem of fitting into a highly organised and very powerful civil service. On the other hand, the committee has to survive in a welter of constitutional and contractual complications, much more elaborate than any the English know. As for the Soviet Union, I have an impression that the correct placing would bring in a good many questions of academic status.

(3) To be any real good, the committee has to possess (or take, as the Tizard Committee took) powers of action. It needs, at the least, the power of inspection and follow-up. If it does not have those, it will be too far from the reality it is trying to decide about, and too far from the people who are supposed to carry out the decisions. Advisory committees, if they are confined to pure advice and never get near the point of action, fade away into a kind of accidie.

As a matter of historical fact, these conditions for an effective committee have quite often been achieved. In any particular case, it ought to be reasonably easy to achieve them again. It is—and this is bad luck for us all—specially easy to do this for military objectives. Military objectives are nearly always more precise than benevolent ones: which is why military technology has been easier for ingenious men to think about.

76   *Science and Government*

Again unfortunately, the constraints of secrecy, though they disturb the comparative judgment, do not disturb the scientific process. In more liberal days, in the days of Rutherford's Cambridge, Bohr's Copenhagen, Franck's Göttingen, scientists tended to assume, as an optimistic act of faith, as something which ought to be true because it made life sweeter, that science could only flourish in the free air.

I wish it were so. I think everyone who has ever witnessed secret science and secret choices wishes it were so. But nearly all the evidence is dead against it. Science needs discussion, yes: it needs the criticism of other scientists: but that can be made to exist, and of course has been made to exist, in the most secret projects. Scientists have worked, apparently happily, and certainly effectively, in conditions which would have been thought the negation of science by the great free-minded practitioners. But the secret, the closed, the climate which to earlier scientists would have been morally intolerable, soon becomes easy to tolerate. I even doubt whether, if one could compare the rate of advance in one of the secret sciences[46] with one of those which is still open to the world, there would be any significant difference. It is a pity.

There is a difference, though, in the rate at which the sciences open to the world get into action. Since those sciences are by definition the ones which cannot

Science and Government   77

be pointed at a military objective, they get into action slower. The exceptions, though perhaps only partial exceptions, are the cluster of sciences which can be applied to medicine. In medicine the objectives are are often as clear-cut as in military science.[47] In fact, there is a certain grim family resemblance. This gives edge and sharpness to the deployment of medical research. For it is not the nature of the objective that makes for speedy action, whether it is destructive or on the side of life. All that matters is that there should be an objective at all.

I am speaking very much as an outsider here, and even if I were not, it is difficult to be sure what one means when one speaks of the efficiency of research and development. But, if that phrase means anything, I should have thought the efficiency of medical research in both the United States and England is a good deal higher than of military research. The choices, often because they are not so much all-or-nothing, have been more sensibly made. This is true, although the administrative techniques in the two countries are not the same. Our Medical Research Council, working with funds Americans would think derisory, is an unusual example, very much admired among people who are studying the arts of government, of a government organ which is acting not so much as a controlling force, but as an impresario.

78 Science and Government

So in military science, and on a lesser scale in medical science, government manages to get some results. But an awful lot of life doesn't consist either of trying to accelerate people's deaths or alternatively to delay them. In the application of science to this vast mid-range of human life, the problems are vaguer, the impetus is less, the pressures of government do not weigh so heavy. A good many benevolent initiatives get lost, although government in the United States, and with slightly less conviction in England, might think that (a) this was not their business, (b) the initiatives will work their way out elsewhere in the society. It is arguable that that is so, but I am by no means convinced. And governments are not convinced either, because they have set out some sort of springboard where these initiatives can get started. In the United States, unless I am wrong, this springboard ought to be provided by the National Research Council. In England, by the Advisory Council on Scientific Policy. In the Soviet Union, by the Academy of Sciences itself, which is a much smaller body than the U. S. National Academy of Sciences or than the Royal Society of London. The Soviet Academy of Sciences is made up of something like 250 full Academicians, and about 150 corresponding members. It contains historians, economists, various kinds of literary scholars, and even creative writers. About 70 per cent are scientists

Science and Government 79

in the restricted Western sense. It is difficult to guess how completely they succeed as a source of scientific initiative. As for us, I do not think anyone would claim that our organs are well-designed for the job.

Does that matter? Is there a job? Hasn't the West in particular got so much applied science in so many quarters that it doesn't need any encouragement?

Does anyone in his senses need more material possessions than the ordinary comfortably off professional American? Or indeed as many? I have some sympathy with anyone who asks me that. And yet, with the ultimate attitude behind it, I haven't so much sympathy after all.

Why not leave well alone? You have said yourself that not many scientists make good administrators. Why worry about science and government? Why not keep the scientists in their place, as we used to, and just call them out to give advice to wiser men?

Isn't the first, the only serious problem of our time, to save the peace? Why does it matter what we do with the scientists? Isn't it the statesman's job to save the peace? What does it matter about scientists?

I am familiar with those questions. They are asked by intelligent men. There is a lot of truth in some of them. And yet they are no good. Or rather, they spring from roots from which spring also many of our dangers and our losses of hope. One of those dangers

80   *Science and Government*

is that we are beginning to shrug off our sense of the future.

This is true all over the West. True even in the United States, though to a lesser extent than in the old societies of Western Europe. We are becoming existential societies—and we are living in the same world with future-directed societies. This existential flavour is obvious in our art. In fact, we are becoming unable to accept any other kind of art. It is there to be seen in quarters much nearer the working mechanism of our society, in the deepest of our administrative arrangements, in the way we make the secret choices that I spoke of at the beginning, in the nature of the secret choices themselves. We seem to be flexible, but we haven't any model of the future before us. In the significant sense, we can't change. And to change is what we have to do.

That is why I want scientists active in all the levels of government. By "scientists" here I mean people trained in the natural sciences, not only engineers, though I want them too. I make a special requirement for the scientists proper, because, partly by training, partly by self-selection, they include a number of speculative and socially imaginative minds. While engineers—more uniform in attitude than one would expect a professional class to be—tend to be technically bold and advanced but at the same time to accept totally any society into which they may have hap-

Science and Government   81

pened to be born. The scientists proper are nothing like so homogeneous in attitude, and some of them will provide a quality which it seems to me we need above everything else.

I do not merely mean here that, if we had scientists of any kind diffused through government, the number of people helping to influence secret choices is bound to increase. That is true. In my view, and it is one of the points from which I started, it would be a real gain. It is a clear advantage to the Soviet Union that they have, right at the top of the political and administrative trees, a fairly high proportion of men with scientific or technical training. The proportion of these men in the top executive organs, or among high-ranking diplomats, seems to be somewhere between 35 and 45 per cent, which is far higher than in the United States or England. In the fields where they have made better technical choices than either of us, and there are plenty, this collective influence has no doubt been a help. But, though that is a real gain, it is secondary to what I have most in mind. I believe scientists have something to give which our kind of existential society is desperately short of: so short of, that it fails to recognise of what it is starved. That is foresight.

I am not saying, of course, that all scientists have foresight and no one else has. Foresight is a fairly rare quality. Mr. Secretary Stimson showed some of it,

82   *Science and Government*

more than other political figures at the time, in his memorandum to President Truman, dated April 25, 1945, about the consequences of the atomic bomb.[48] But compare the kind of prescience in this memorandum with that of Franck and the Chicago scientists in their famous letter ten weeks later.

Stimson had to rely on his political sense. Franck and his colleagues had training and something which we can loosely call knowledge behind them. It was not quite knowledge. It was much more an expectation of knowledge to come. It was something that a scientist, if he has this kind of sensitivity latent in him, picks up during his scientific experience.

I believe it is something we grossly undervalue: rather like paleolithic men, before arithmetic had been invented, jeering at someone who had a knack of counting on his fingers. I suppose most scientists possess nothing of this foresight. But, if they have any trace of the capability, then their experience, more than any experience at present open to us, gives them the chance to bring it out. For science, by its very nature, exists in history. Any scientist realises that his subject is moving in time—that he knows incomparably more today than better, cleverer, and deeper men did twenty years ago. He knows that his pupils, in twenty years, will know incomparably more than he does. Scientists have it within them to know what a

Science and Government   83

future-directed society feels like, for science itself, in its human aspect, is just that.

That is my deepest reason for wanting scientists in government. I have tried a shot at an explanation why in their youth they are often not good at the arts of administration. As one thinks back to the operations of the Tizard Committee, it is worth remembering that their decisions were carried out by professional administrators. If these had been replaced by scientists, the scientists would almost certainly have done worse.

But that is only half of it. I spent twenty years of my life in close contact with the English professional administrators. I have the greatest respect for them—more respect, I think, than for any professional group I know. They are extremely intelligent, honourable, tough, tolerant, and generous. Within the human limits, they are free from some of the less pleasing group characteristics. But they have a deficiency.

Remember, administrators are by temperament active men. Their tendency, which is strengthened by the nature of their job, is to live in the short term, to become masters of the short-term solution. Often, as I have seen them conducting their business with an absence of fuss, a concealed force, a refreshing dash of intellectual sophistication, a phrase from one of the old Icelandic sagas kept nagging at my mind. It was: "Snorri was the wisest man in Iceland who had not the gift of foresight."[49]

84 *Science and Government*

Foresight in this quotation meant something supernatural, but nevertheless the phrase stayed with me. The wisest man who had not the gift of foresight. The more I have seen of Western societies, the more it nags at me. It nags at me in the United States, just as in Western Europe. We are immensely competent; we know our own pattern of operations like the palm of our hands. It is not enough. That is why I want some scientists mixed up in our affairs. It would be bitter if, when this storm of history is over, the best epitaph that anyone could write of us was only that: "The wisest men who had not the gift of foresight."

NOTES

T. P. means Tizard Papers.

1. Don K. Price, *Government and Science* (New York University Press, New York, 1954), p. 30. Much the most interesting and experienced book on the subject that I have read. Nothing written on government and science in England remotely compares with it.
2. T. P., diary, May 8, 1945.
3. T. P., autobiography, MS, p. 17.
4. House of Lords Hansard, 1957, weekly No. 323, pp.

Notes 85

482–496. He was referring to an article of mine in the *New Statesman* called "New Minds for the New World" (Sept. 6, 1956). As I was still in Government employment at the time, my friends in Whitehall preferred me not to sign this article; but the authorship was an open secret.

5. R. F. Harrod, *The Prof* (Macmillan, London, 1959), pp. 15, 107. Sir Roy Harrod's book is a biographical memoir of Lindemann. Harrod knew his subject intimately, but would not claim to understand Lindemann's scientific life.

6. T. P., autobiography, MS, p. 52.

7. *Ibid.*, p. 66.

8. *Ibid.*, p. 122.

9. *Ibid.*, p. 124.

10. F. W. Aston spent years of his life developing the mass spectrograph, and Wilson years of his on the cloud chamber: both were Nobel prize winners. Sir Thomas Merton is a distinguished spectroscopist and, incidentally, a distinguished art connoisseur and collector.

11. He had become second-in-command to Bertram Hopkinson, who was in effect head of aircraft research. Hopkinson, the most eminent academic engineer of his generation, was killed piloting his own aircraft in 1918: he, more than anyone, taught Tizard what military science meant.

12. One can, of course, make psychological guesses. It would be fairly easy to make plausible guesses about both Roosevelt-Hopkins and Churchill-Lindemann.

13. Rowe played an important part, easy to underestimate because the whole of it was secret, in the scientific war, 1935–45. He is best known as the superintendent of the Telecommunication Research Establishment, the most brilliant and successful of the English wartime research establishments.

86 Notes

14. It is worth noticing that Wimperis, who was a peace-loving, sweet-natured man, ill-at-ease among violent disputes, both got the committee going and selected Tizard.

15. In 1948.

16. Lord Swinton's part in these preparations, like Rowe's, though for different reasons, has been constantly underestimated.

17. At this time Sir Maurice, later Lord, Hankey. One of the great invisible influences in English affairs, particularly military affairs, for a generation. His part has not yet been properly described.

18. Later head of the Civil Service and now Lord Bridges.

19. Cf. P. M. S. Blackett, "Tizard and the Science of War," *Nature 185*, 647–653 (1960).

20. "Operations research" in the United States. But the English started it, and I much prefer the English name. In the 1914–18 war, A. V. Hill's scientists were testing anti-aircraft gunnery and were carrying out what we should later have called operational research.

21. P. M. S. Blackett, "Operational Research," *Brassey's Annual* (1953), 88–106.

22. Cf. W. S. Churchill, *The Second World War* (Cassell, London, 1948), vol. 1, pp. 399–401, 593–594.

23. Not 1937 as stated in Churchill, p. 120. There are other inaccuracies in the chapter ("Problems of Sea and Air, 1935–1939," pp. 115–128).

24. This is Blackett's account. Rowe is inclined to think, without being certain, that this critical quarrel took place before a meeting. It may easily have happened that, since a row was expected, the secretaries were told not to come in at the beginning.

25. Except Hankey. That most discreet of men, who

Notes 87

never let slip a secret in his life, thought this was the time to do so.

26. T. P., diary, May 10, 11, 1940. R. A. E. is the Royal Aircraft Establishment; A. I. is air interception; C. H. is the first-stage chain interception; G. L. is the training of searchlights in combination with anti-aircraft guns.

27. T. P., diary, June 4, 1940.

28. *Ibid.*, June 7, 1940. S. of S. is Secretary of State.

29. *Ibid.*, June 21, 1940. C. A. S. is Chief of Air Staff.

30. *Ibid.*, July 30, 1940. M. A. P. is Ministry of Aircraft Production.

31. *Ibid.*, August 1, 1940.

32. The magnetron is a device for producing beams of high-frequency radio waves. All the advances in radar after 1940 depended upon it.

33. Blackett, "Tizard and the Science of War," loc. cit.

34. Harrod, *The Prof*, pp. 74–75, had clearly not been told the nature of the argument, either in this matter or (pp. 176–178) in the prewar quarrel.

35. The controversy would have had to be submitted with a large amount of factual background, such as the way in which aircraft are actually operated in practice. It was precisely in the misuse of this factual background that Lindemann's statistics went wrong.

36. That is, of the independent scientific members, Wimperis and Rowe were also on Tizard's side.

37. *The New Men* (Macmillan, London, 1954), pp. 278–279.

38. An interesting field of investigation would be the British Broadcasting Corporation, which, despite the Kafka-like impression it makes on outsiders, must provide some textbook examples of hierarchical politics.

39. There is a story that a small deputation of Fellows of the Royal Society called on Churchill and said that

88 Notes

they distrusted Lindemann's scientific judgment. It would have made a pleasing scene; but I have, with regret, satisfied myself that the story is not true.

40. Some examples of these political processes enter into my novels, cf. *The Masters, The New Men, Homecomings, The Affair.*

41. I owe this remark, which seems to me truer the more I think of it, to Pamela Hansford Johnson.

42. *The Two Cultures and the Scientific Revolution* (Cambridge University Press, Cambridge, 1959). This was the Rede Lecture for 1959.

43. I am using "gadget" to mean any practical device, from an egg beater to a hydrogen bomb. The kind of mind which is fascinated by the one is likely to be fascinated by the other.

44. Rowe, who saw more of the English scientific choices between 1935 and 1945 than any single man, is inclined to think that, of all the scientists he met, Lindemann had the worst judgment. Judgment, that is, of science applied to war. (Letter to C. P. S., Aug. 3, 1960.)

45. They did not feel this, of course, about Tizard himself.

46. That is, those parts of science which are directly applicable to war.

47. It is, of course, also true that the feeling of society is deeply involved in military and medical science, and lays great stress upon them. If a similar stress were laid on the problems of transport, we might get scientific solutions quite quickly.

48. Cf. Elting E. Morison's biography of Stimson, *Turmoil and Tradition* (Houghton Mifflin, Boston, 1960), pp. 613–643.

49. *Saga of Burnt Njal,* chapter 113. "Foresight" in modern translations sometimes appears as "prescience."